Our American Family™

I Am Italian American

Brenda DePalma

The Rosen Publishing Group's
PowerKids Press™
New York

To Len—the best husband and research assistant an author ever had.

Published in 1997 by The Rosen Publishing Group, Inc.
29 East 21st Street, New York, NY 10010

First Edition

Book Design: Erin McKenna

Photo Credits: Cover and p. 4 © Dusty Willison/International Stock Photo; p. 7 © Hilary Wilkes/International Stock; p. 8 © International Stock Photo; pp. 11, 12 © FPG International Corp; p. 15 © Mark Bolster/International Stock Photo; p. 16 © Ryan Williams/International Stock Photo; p. 19 © Miwako Ikeda/International Stock Photo; p. 20 © Peter Krinninger/International Stock Photo.

DePalma, Brenda.
    I am Italian American / by Brenda DePalma.
        p.   cm. — (Our American Family)
    Includes index.
    Summary: An Italian-American child talks about aspects of his Italian heritage, including famous Italians, foods, and traditions.
    ISBN 0-8239-5015-8
    1. Italian Americans—Juvenile literature. [1. Italian Americans.]
    I. Title. II. Series.
E184.I8T86 1997
973'.0451—dc21
                                          96-54019
                                            CIP
                                            AC

Manufactured in the United States of America

Contents

Joey

My name is Joseph, but everybody calls me Joey. I live in Philadelphia, Pennsylvania. I have three older sisters and two older brothers. We live in a brownstone apartment building. My grandparents live in a brownstone next door. I see them every day after school. I also see them on Sunday mornings, when we all go to church together. We go to a Roman Catholic church.

◀ You can learn a lot about your heritage by talking to your family.

Italy

My grandparents came to the United States many years ago from a country in Europe called Italy. On a map, Italy looks like a high-heeled boot. More than 60 million people live there. Some of them live in little towns and villages. Others live in big cities. My family is from a city in southern Italy called Napoli, or Naples.

Many Italians have dark skin and dark hair. Some have fair skin and blond or light brown hair. Everyone in my family has brown hair and brown eyes.

The Colosseum was built in Rome between 72 and 81 A.D. It is one of the most famous sites in the world. ▶

Columbus Day

Christopher Columbus was an Italian explorer who believed there were other lands beyond Europe. Many people didn't believe him. So on August 3, 1492, Columbus set sail with his three ships, the Niña, the Pinta, and the Santa Maria in search of the "New World." On October 12, 1492, his ships landed in America. Christopher Columbus had found the New World!

Today, October 12 is a national holiday. Italian Americans are very proud of Christopher Columbus.

One of the ships used by Columbus and his crew was the Santa Maria. A model of the ship can be seen here.

Mother Cabrini

In school I did a report on a famous Italian American named Mother Cabrini.

Frances Xavier Cabrini liked helping people. She worked as a teacher and at an **orphanage** (OR-fen-ej). In 1880, she started a **missionary order** (MISH-un-eh-ree OR-der) for nuns in Italy. Mother Cabrini made 37 trips to the United States, bringing nuns with her to help the poor. During one of these trips, Mother Cabrini became an American citizen. She also helped Italian **immigrants** (IM-ih-grentz) settle in the United States.

Mother Cabrini died in 1917. She was the first U.S. citizen to be named a saint. ▶

On to America

In the early 1900s, hard times fell on the farmers of Italy. Rich men had taken over their farms. Often, a whole family was forced to work on land that now belonged to other people. For their work, many Italian families were allowed to keep a small part of the harvested crop.

But hardworking farmers still couldn't support their families. They didn't have enough money or food. So they decided to leave their country and go to the United States, hoping for a better life.

◀ The first thing that many Italian immigrants saw when they arrived in the United States was the Statue of Liberty.

13

The Feast of San Gennaro

Last September my family and I went to New York City to the Feast of San Gennaro, or Festa di San Gennaro. It is the oldest and largest festival honoring the Italian saint, Saint Gennaro.

For eleven days over 3 million people go to Mott Street in Little Italy to taste wonderful Italian food. There's pasta, pizza, and more desserts than you can imagine! I like to eat the sausage and pepper sandwich, which is piled high with lots of onions.

During the San Gennaro Festival, people who aren't Italian American can get a taste of Italian culture on the streets of Little Italy. ▶

Geraldine Ferraro

Geraldine Ferraro was a teacher in New York. She also went to law school. She studied hard, and became a lawyer. She fought against crime in New York. But Geraldine wanted to do more. In 1978 she was elected to Congress. Six years later, Geraldine was **nominated** (NOM-in-ay-ted) for the position of vice president of the United States. She was the first Italian American and the first woman ever to be nominated.

Geraldine did not win the election. But she still plays an important role in politics.

My mother admires Geraldine Ferraro and her hard work. Mom says Geraldine is a smart and strong Italian American woman. I think so too.

17

Mangia!

Every Sunday, my family makes dinner together. My sister often makes chicken or fish with oregano and garlic. My dad makes a sauce for our pasta. We all take turns stirring the tomato sauce that cooks in a big pot on the stove. My father got the recipe from his mother, who brought it to the United States from Italy. There are many different kinds of pasta dishes. My favorite is **manicotti** (MAN-ih-COT-ee). My grandparents often eat with us. They say *"Mangia!"* or *"Eat!"*

18

Pasta comes in many different shapes and sizes. This shape is called penne. ▶

Wine

My older sister, Lily, worked on a **vineyard** (VIN-yerd) in Italy last summer. Italian wine is some of the most flavorful wine in the world. Lily told me the grapes are grown on vines in the rich soil. When they are ripe, the grapes are picked, pressed, and the juice is put in big barrels. The juice sits for a long time until it **ferments** (FER-ments). Then it is put into bottles and shipped around the world. My sister said she learned a lot while she was at the **winery** (WYN-er-ee).

◀ Vineyards can be found all over Italy. Some Italian winemakers brought their grapes from Italy and started vineyards in the United States.

I Am Italian American

I like to learn about my **heritage** (HEHR-ih-tij). My grandmother tells me stories about what it was like to grow up in Italy. My father shows me how to measure the right amounts of spices for the tomato sauce. I learn about famous Italian Americans in school. I see the Italian American actor Al Pacino and the singer and actress Madonna in movies and on TV. I am learning more and more every day about who I am and where my family is from. I am proud to be Italian American.

Glossary

ferment (FER-ment) A chemical change where the sugar from fruit is changed into alcohol.

heritage (HEHR-ih-tij) The customs and beliefs that are handed down from parent to child.

immigrant (IM-ih-grent) A person who comes from another country to live in a new one.

manicotti (MAN-ih-COT-ee) Tube-shaped pasta shells that are filled with cheese or meat and are usually covered with tomato sauce.

missionary order (MISH-un-eh-ree OR-der) A group of people who go to other cities or countries and help people in need.

nominate (NOM-in-ayt) To suggest someone for a position.

orphanage (OR-fen-ej) A home for children whose parents have died.

vineyard (VIN-yerd) An area where grape vines are planted.

winery (WYN-er-ee) A place where wine is made.

Index